YOU WILL LOVE THIS

PRERNA DHINGRA

ISBN 979-888530947-9

I dedicate this book to every one out there who would like to join
me in a new and amazing journey.

Contents

Foreword

The soothing embrace of breeze, faint rustle of leaves, refreshing scent of soil just after it has rained - it takes you deep down the lane of memories. You feel like you belong somewhere - with nature. The stabbing pain of anger, helplessness when nobody is there to support you - we all have been there.

Nature is abundant joy. Nature is bliss. Nature is magical. Everyone's childhood, teenage, adulthood, everyone's life is connected to nature. We can't just ignore how magical the world is we live in and unfortunately, this fact too that it's slowly getting destroyed - which most of us cannot see right now but the future generations will unless we do something.

In this collection, I have captured the stunning beauty of nature. After a lot of thinking, I chose to write down most of my experiences also considering eveything to be a part of nature and to share it with all of my wonderful readers.

Prerna Dhingra

1. Weather Of Dreams

Land was being heated like the Sun, all were falling ill because of cruel heat, some were planning to leave and go;
sitting under the cool shade of tree,
I was contemplating - what to do.
Suddenly, a change came in the weather, birds started fluttering their feathers, sound of thunder struck my ears, scampering squirrels 'n rabbits hid cause of fear.
As far as I could see, clouds covered the endless sky, wind screamed and clouds began to cry; water poured down, the Earth cooled down, that earlier fried.
Trees and plants began to sing, monkeys on branches swinged, I left my place and went in rain, a drop fell on me and calmed my brain.
I opened my eyes and realised; the sky was blue, the Sun still bright, I saw a man standing beside a dried stream, looking towards the sky who screamed: "Oh God, please again fill up this stream."
Sighing, to myself I thought *who knows I have enjoyed the weather of dreams in my beautiful and peaceful dream.*

2. Forest

• 2 •

In the forest was peace, I could hear only breeze, 'twas gently rustling leaves, of strong enormous trees.

Silently, river was flowing, thump-thump elephants going, to their nests birds hurried and small beings scurried.

Insects roamed everywhere, at night, owls glared. The nights in forest were cold, despite being alone, I wasn't bored.

All around calm silence, ventured without guidance; I found my way, through those enormous trees, where nothing could be heard, except peaceful breeze.

3. Autumn

The soil is not visible,

for the ground is orange,

even the road that cuts through the

middle of those trees, a deserted passage,

Isn't excluded from the shedding of trees' storage;

To fall down and meet the ground, they were longing.

The breeze with the scent of branches

helped in their falling.

Walking through that forest a person, in mind was wishing:

Never go down, O Sun, for I want this evening to last foever,

this Autumn

4. My Anger

It was piercing me every moment, the words were giving rise to anger latent, it was spreading in me like forest fire, ready to kill all like General Dyer.

It was a sign of imminent explosion, which was likely to cause massive destruction, the words did the work of anger construction, later on which resulted in a volcanic eruption.

I was screaming, I was trying, to prevent my brain from frying! But like counting hair, impossible it was, to control that anger, Oh God! It was spreading in me like forest fire, ready to kill all like General Dyer.

5. Hypnotic Beauty

•5•

Soothing sound of peaceful stream, the birds around chirping, brown and orange trees, breeze moving swiftly through their leaves.

Nature is giving so much peace, then a short lived sensation that's gloomy, this scenery heals through it's calming, hypnotic, beauty.

6. Nature

Nature taught me everything;
to learn and how to think:
Birds taught me how to sing,
fishes taught me how to swim,
storms made me valiant,
forests made me reticent.
From oceans, rivers bought me peace,
serious, I was made by the Seas,
landslides made me gallant,
Sun, Moon, made me diligent,
horses taught me how to run,
fire taught me how to burn.
Animals made me rambunctious,
plants made me courteous,
I am grateful to nature,
which developed my character!

7. Serenity

Blue water of lake shined,
in the morning sunlight,
the flowers were bright,
it was a beautiful sight.
I had never seen,
a place so beautiful and serene,
where birds in sky sail,
amid the beautiful vales.
In the winter, you'll see snow,
and after rain, a rainbow.
The trees are sturdy, strong,
and green, muddy, ponds.
You'll love to sit here,
on slopes, without fear.
The sky looks crystal clear,
and the river is near.
Every mountain is green,
it's true, nature is serene.

8. Selective Mutism

"Selective mutism is a severe anxiety disorder where a person is unable to speak in certain social situations, such as with classmates at school or to relatives they do not see very often. It usually starts during childhood and, if left untreated, can persist into adulthood." - NHS UK

Sitting in your class, or in a hotel at the corner,

People think you're shy,

But they don't know it's a disorder

Each time you want to speak,

Your mouth just won't open,

You want to speak so bad but something obstructs.

No one Just gives a chance or takes in my mind

That it takes longer,

To utter a word compared to those who think they're normal

Anywhere, the moment I step out of my home

I am frozen

People think you're spazzer, expressionless, with no emotions

Want to get out of this zone, but the throat's too tight,

To get your voice heard is a cold war fight,

To speak or not is never a choice,

I have selective mustim which makes it hard for me to speak,

it's full of extreme discomfort

9. Most Beautiful Sight

I like to linger in the field,

on top of the mount,

can't express how joyful I feel,

when I hear birds' sound.

When I'm surrounded by flowers,

when it drizzles and it showers,

mesmerised by it's beauty,

Earth's scent, oh, how wonderful,

fruits are ever so juicy.

Everything guarded by pine towers,

surrounded by the aroma of blooming flowers,

deep in the forest, away from hustle-bustle,

undisturbed to look at leaves rustle.

Little, merry leaves, of plants, herbs, trees,

dance freely with the breeze.

When I see icy-cold rivers,

imagining how cold it is, it makes me shiver.

When a river in the forest, you find,

it gives real peace of mind.

Gazing at twinkling stars in the night,

is the most beautiful sight.

10. Divine Weather

Crisp leaves scattered all over the ground,
walk over the place, you'll hear a sound;
Just like someone has broken a bundle of sticks,
and the breeze is soothing and swift.
The divine presence of weather touches the soul,
this aura, can only be felt, gives peace more.
Enjoy the moment while it's there,
making yourself comfy with nature's company,
you're not alone, Moon is with you, even the Sun,
that's sunny, squirrels and bunnies.